You Are My SonShines

You Are My SonShines

Atlanta GA

You Are My SONshines
Copyright © 2020 by Winsome Sinclair

All rights reserved. No part of this book may be used or reproduced in any manner whatsoever without written permission except in the case of brief quotations embodied in critical articles or reviews.

First Edition: November 2020

ISBN: 978-0-578-65304-4

For information contact:
Winsome Sinclair
Atlanta, GA

Email: YouAreMySONshine@gmail.com

Illustrations by Maidah Khizar

Printed in the United States of America.

DEDICATION

For my Supernatural sons, Micah & Kairo My SONshines and all the blessed adoptive families that are born of the heart.

Hi my name is MICAH and I am 6 years old. My little brother is KAIRO and he is 4.
They call me Batman. I love playing video games.

Hi I'm KAIRO… I Love dinosaurs…
MICAH is my big brother.
They call me Elmo.

This is our mommy SOMEY and she is the best mommy and she is Boss. She says she loves us more than anything in the world.

We love our mommy This MUCH. She says we were made for each other and we are her SONshines. Mom says we are blessed and GOD formed our family in a supernatural non-traditional way.

We like to do fun things with our mommy, like riding our bikes in the park. My bike is blue, Kairo's bike is red. We ride very fast and mommy watches us from the bench.

Sometimes we dance and sing with each other. MOMMY says our favorite music is "old skool".

We also love to eat. Sometimes MOMMY lets us help her in the kitchen when she prepares our meals. Tuna fish sandwiches are our favorite meal to eat. Mommy says I might be a chef when I grow up.

After we eat we love to help MOMMY clean up. She teaches us so many new things. We love being MOMMY's little helpers.

Mommy says we are the best helpers EVER!!!

Mommy takes us to school every morning. We like to sing along with her and the music on the radio. Kairo and I go to different schools.

At night MOMMY helps us with our homework. I am learning to read and use a laptop. We love to learn. Kairo tries to always copy me. Mommy says we are both super smart.

Sometimes mommy takes us to basketball practice. She says the coach thinks I'm very good.

We also love gymnastics. Kairo loves to do cartwheels. Mommy says soon we will start Karate classes as well.

Mommy says that we are very special. She says that we are her supernatural babies. Blessed by GOD and born of her heart.

MOMMY also says that she is glad that KAIRO and I talked to GOD and chose her to be our MOMMY. KAIRO and I Love when MOMMY prays with us every night. This is how we talk to GOD. This is when we thank GOD for each other, and all the people that love us.

Mommy says that we are her SONshines and are especially loved by GOD and by her.

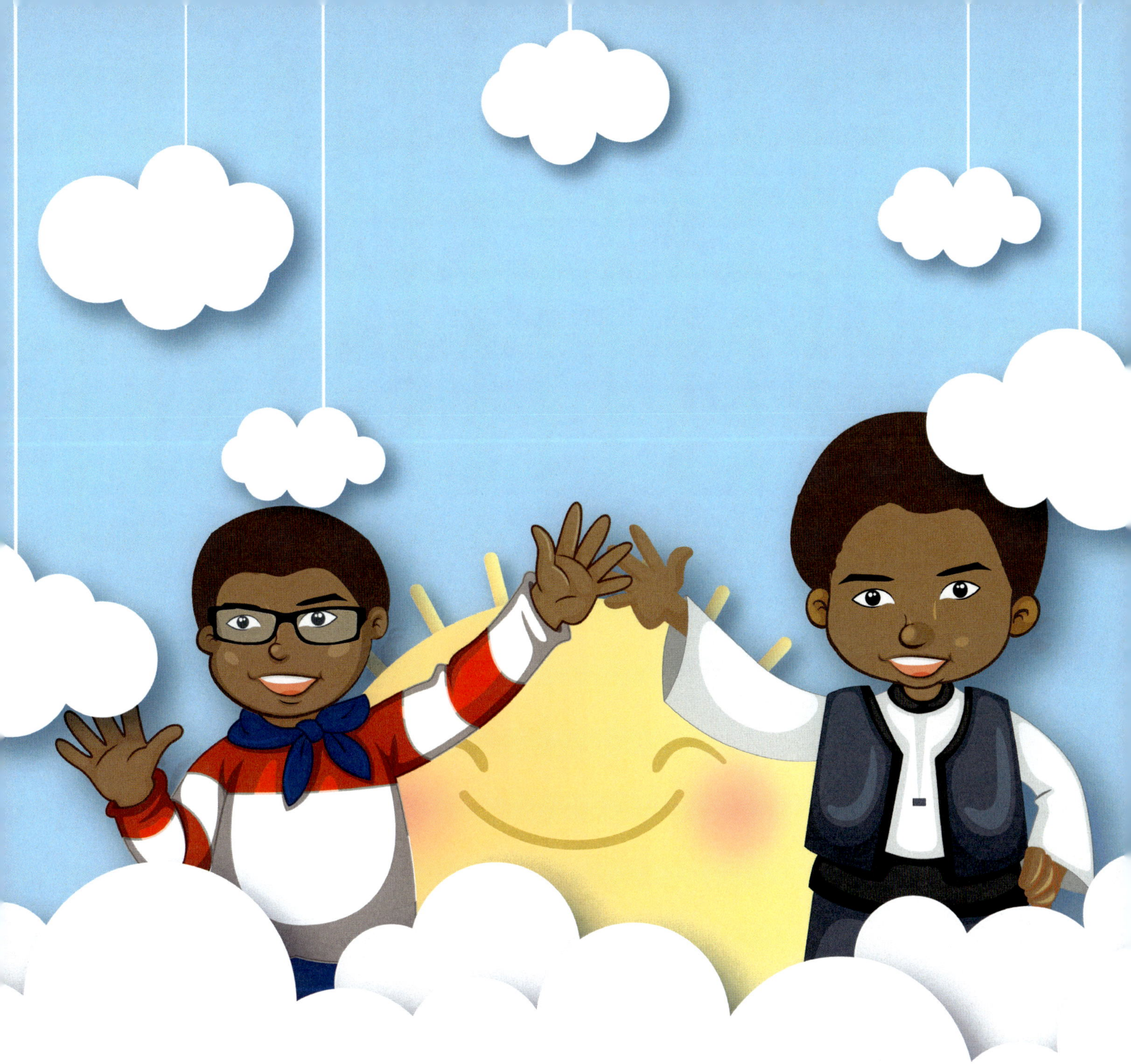

We were born of mommy's heart through prayers.

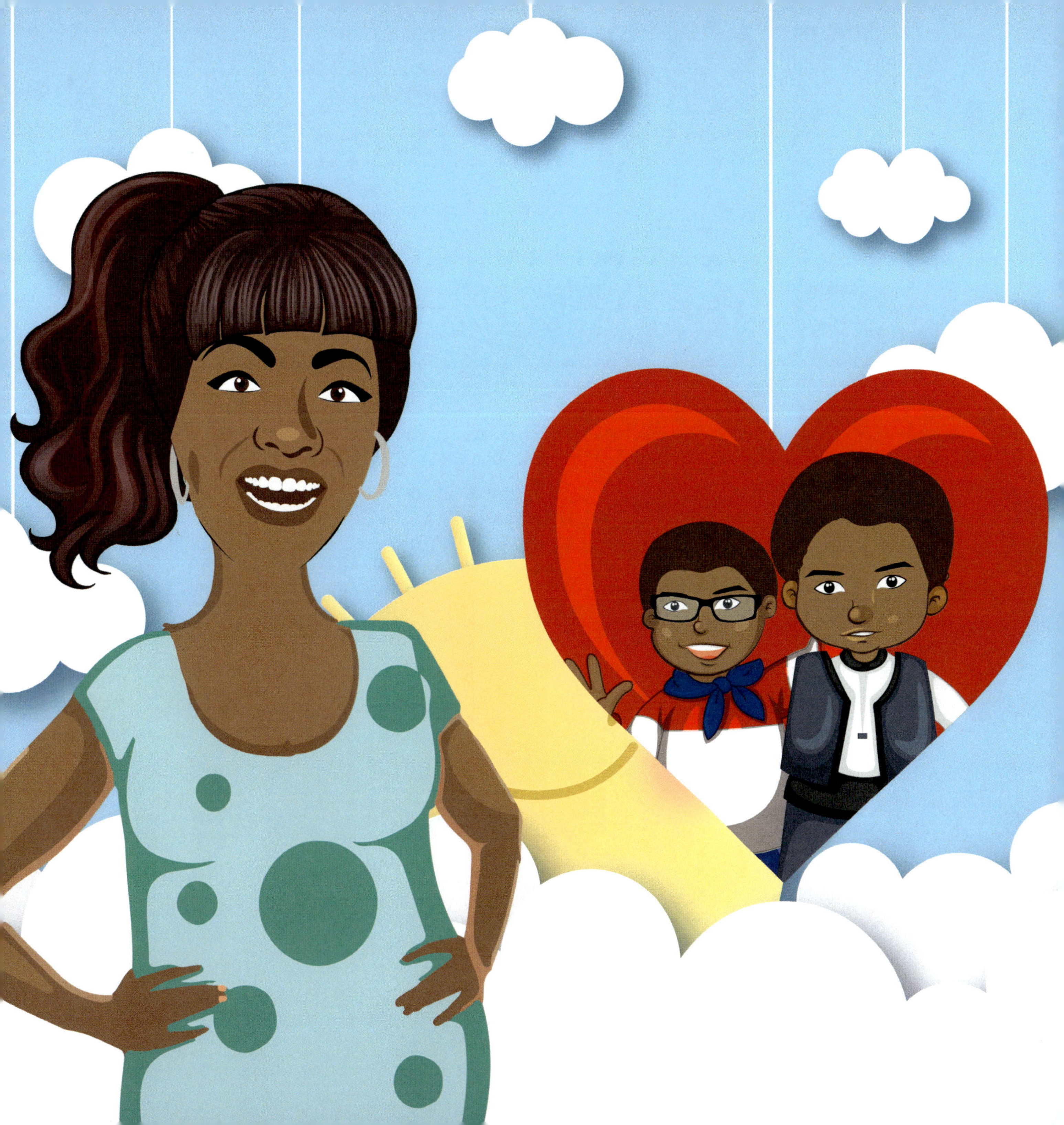

GOD knew we needed each other and heard all 3 of our prayers.

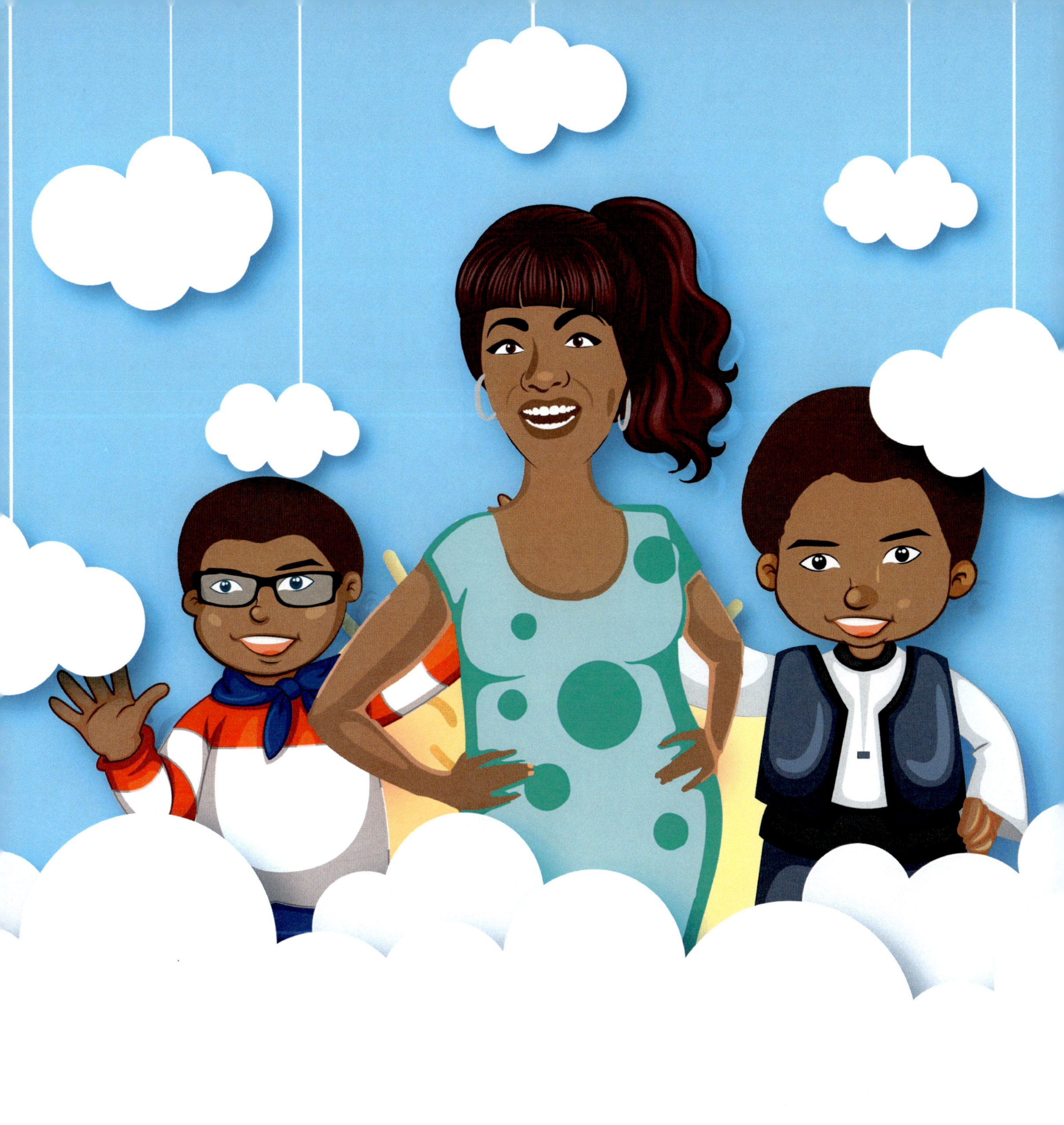

We are part of a big family. Mommy says it takes a village to raise us. Our village includes: our grandparents, god parents, uncles, aunts, and cousins. We love our family.

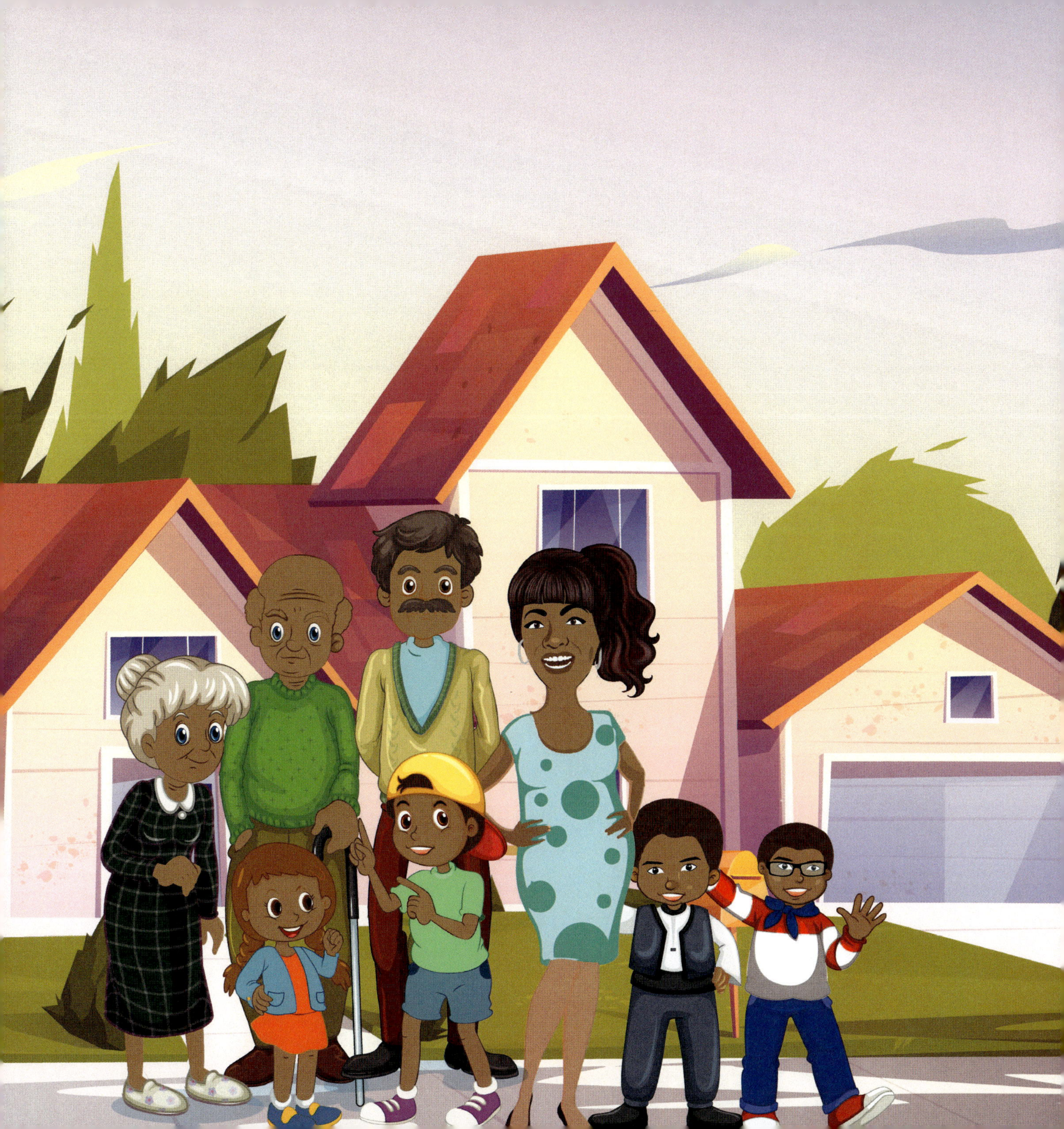

We are grateful that GOD answers prayers, and made our dreams of having a family come true. Every night we pray that GOD blesses other families to find each other the way we did.. Mommy says some families are traditional, but we are supernatural.

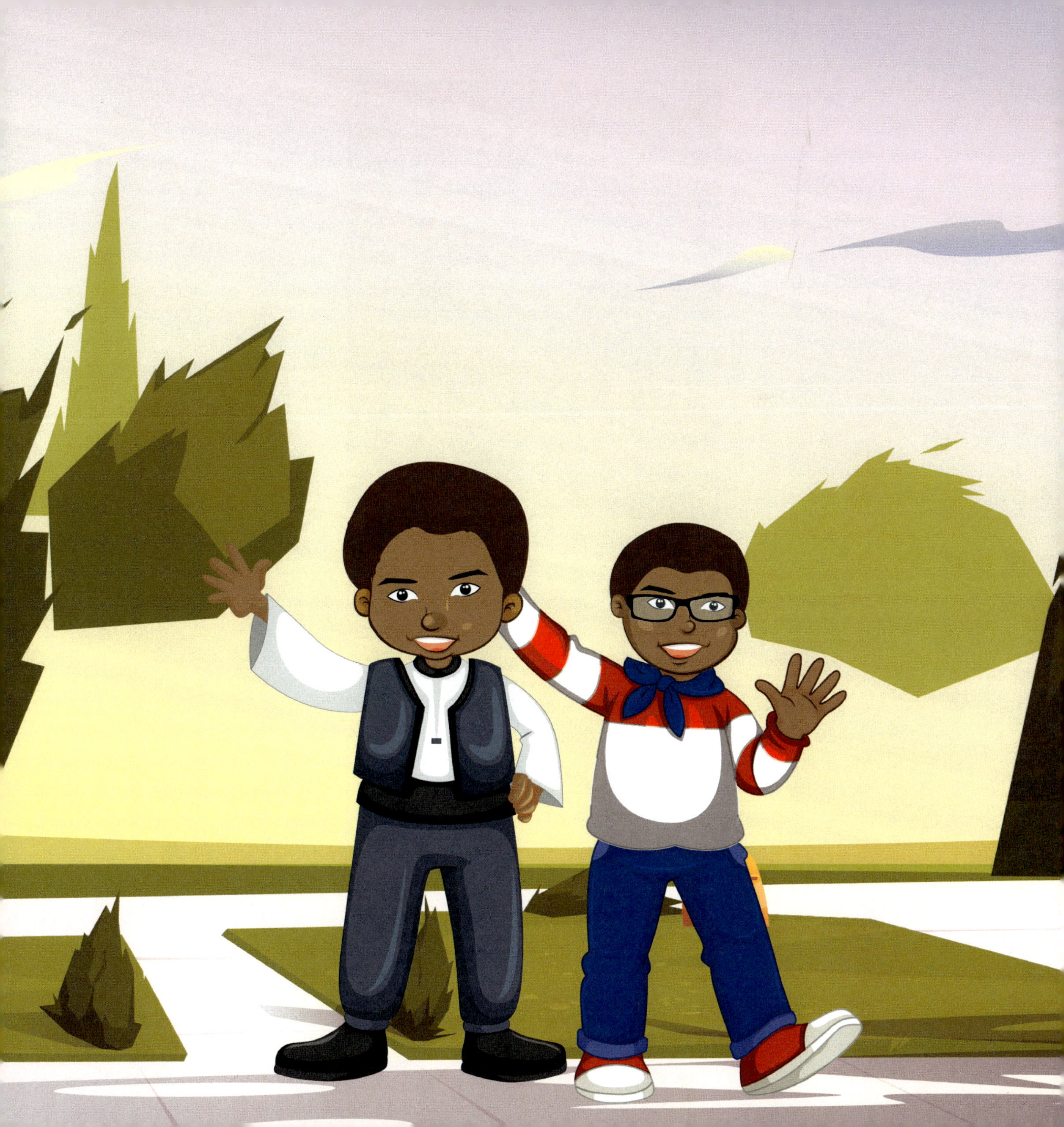

Casting Director | Producer
Public Speaker

Winsome Sinclair is a highly respected casting director and founder of the glob-al casting agency, Winsome Sinclair and Associates.

A graduate of Florida A&M University, Winsome began her film and television career under the tutelage of film director, Spike Lee. From the late 80s through the 2000s, she collaborated with Spike on all feature film projects for 23 years. In 1996, Sinclair set out on her own business path by laying entrepreneurial roots in her home state of New York through her namesake company, Winsome Sinclair and Associates.

To date, the firm has collaborated with such directors as Steven Spielberg, Spike Lee, Oliver Stone, John Singleton and Lee Daniels. Over the years, WSA has also joined forces with others casting principals and/or extras for major box office films like Amistad, Malcolm X, Waiting to Exhale, The Best Man, In-side Man, Too Fast Too Furious, Black Snake Moan, Cadillac Records, Sparkle, Precious and many others.

Made in the USA
Columbia, SC
02 November 2021